THE BATTLE of the B★A★N★D★S

NEIL HUDDLESTONE

illustrated by Jo Langley

GINN

Contents

Chapter One

Solo Street

There are three bands in our street. How can one street be so lucky, says my mother.

Sophy Harris lives at Number 5. Her band is called Sophy and the Songbirds. The Songbirds are three of her mates from school. They sing all these droopy love songs. They think they're great.

Number 15 is our house. My brother, Darren, has a band called the Heartbeats. Darren plays the lead guitar. They have a big red heart with lights around it. The lights flash on and off. The girls love it.

It's a funny thing to say about your own brother but Darren's really nice. Some boys tease their sisters. Darren never teases me. All he cares about is music. He's always making up new tunes.

Across the road at Number 18 live Brad Morgan and his brother, Rick. Their band is called the Chain Gang. Rick can't play but he does the lights. On stage the band wear plastic balls and chains around their legs.

I don't like Brad. He's mean. Once he dropped a burning match in my gumboot. He did it on purpose. He picks on the girl in the milk bar, too. He gives her five dollars. Then he says he gave her ten dollars and he makes her give him more change. Brad can't make up tunes the way Darren can. He copies his music from tapes and records.

"You be careful of Brad," I say to Darren. "He's mean. He takes your songs."

"Don't you worry, Lisa," Darren says. "Brad's a good bloke really."

Chapter Two

The Scout Hall

It can get pretty noisy in our street. The shop on the corner has a big sign that says, "GET YOUR EARPLUGS HERE! LOW PRICES!" People are always ringing the estate agent to ask for quieter places.

"What about the graveyard?" he says. "That's quiet. People are dying to get in there."

One day I was walking along playing my
radio. Old Mr Hunt stuck his head out the
window.

"If I don't get some peace, young
woman," he yelled, "I'll grab that radio and
jump on it!" As if! He talks like that but he
doesn't mean it.

What with all the noise and people sending Dad bills for their earmuffs, the Heartbeats began to practise in the Northside Scout Hall.

The Scout Hall is behind a row of shops. It has a lane on one side and a parking lot on the other. The windows are small and barred. The door has a big bolt and a padlock. Brad didn't like Darren using the Scout Hall. It made it harder for him to copy Darren's music. Sometimes I saw Brad's car parked in the lane. Sometimes he came in.

"I heard a cat howling," he'd say. "So I came to save the poor thing." He thinks that's funny.

One time I went out to buy some Cokes.
When I came back Brad was in the porch.
He was sliding the bolt on the door to and
fro and turning the key in the lock.

"What are you doing?" I asked.
Brad jumped. He went red.
"I'm minding my own business, girlie,"
he snapped. "Why don't you mind yours?"
I hate it when he calls me "girlie".

Chapter Three

Northside Council meets

One day Northside Council had a big meeting. One of the councillors, Mr Sharpe, said something should be done for the youth of the district.

"Something like what?" asked the other council members.

"Something like a Battle of the Bands," said Mr Sharpe. Mr Sharpe owns a music store.

"We don't want any battles in Northside," said Mr Nockett. "This is a quiet suburb."

"Not if you live in Solo Street," said Mr Sharpe. "We will have a big contest in the Town Hall. It will show the other suburbs how good we are. We will have four judges and a big prize."

"Where are we going to get the money?" asked Mr Nockett.

"We will ask Channel Four to show the winning band on TV," said Mr Sharpe. "This will be a great prize and it will not cost us a cent."

The council was very pleased with this idea.

"But," said Mrs Agatha Whalebone, "I have seen some of these bands. Their clothes are torn. They have tattoos and long hair. Northside will be overrun by thugs."

"Never fear, dear lady," said Mr Sharpe. "This contest will be only for the people of Northside."

"In that case," said Mrs Whalebone, "I will be a judge. I like music. My late husband played the bagpipes."

"I will be a judge too," said Mr Sharpe. "After all, it was my idea."

"We want someone who knows something about it," said Mr Nockett.

So the judges were Mrs Whalebone, Mr Sharpe, pop star Susie Blue, and Troy Todman, the host of Channel Four's music show.

Chapter Four

Locked in!

When the news broke, the sales of earplugs rose all over Northside.

Brad bought a new set of drums. Darren went to work on a new song. Sophy and the Songbirds made new dresses.

So many bands went in for the Battle that heats had to be held. The timetable of these heats was very strict. If a band did not turn up, it was crossed out.

Before their heat, Darren and the boys had a final practice in the Scout Hall. I went to the Town Hall to see the fun.

The hall was full of noise and people. Lights were flashing. Bands were warming up. Girls were dancing. Brad and his gang were there. But where was Darren?

Brad saw me.

"Hey Lisa," he called, "Darren's cutting it fine. If he's late he'll miss out."

"He'll be here," I said, but I was worried.
The Chain Gang belted out their hit
number. Rick made the lighting look like
prison bars. With the balls and chains it
looked good.

Then it was Darren's turn. The judge called for the Heartbeats. No answer. The judge called again.

"He's been held up!" I called. Darren's
car must have had a smash, I thought.
Nothing else would keep him away. The
judge crossed the Heartbeats off the board.

"Next," he called.

Two more bands played. Then the speaker said that band Number 7 had pulled out. At that very moment, the Heartbeats rushed in to the hall.

"We will take Number 7's place!" called Darren. The boys jumped onto the stage. You should have seen Brad's face!

"They're breaking the rules," he said, but no-one heard.

Luckily, their near miss didn't stop the Heartbeats from playing well. They won a place in the final. The Chain Gang and the Songbirds made it to the final, too.

"What went wrong?" I asked Darren later. "It was lucky for you that band pulled out."

"We were locked in the Scout Hall," said Darren. "Someone bolted the door and pushed the padlock shut. I didn't think we would ever get out."

"Who was it?" I asked.

"Some idiot," said Darren. "If I catch him, I'll tie his legs around his neck."

I thought of Brad playing with the key. I was sure he had locked Darren in. It was just the sort of thing he would do.

Chapter Five

Brad tries again

After that I was sure Brad wanted to put Darren out of the Battle of the Bands. I watched him every time he came to our place. I knew he would try again. But how?

On the day of the final, Darren checked all the band's gear. The guitars. The leads and plugs. The pedals. These pedals change the sound of the instruments. They are different colours — blue, yellow and red. Darren has three pedals. Brad has four. Big bands have about ten.

Darren was putting the gear into the van when Brad and Rick came over. Here they come, I thought. Brad will pull a trick now.

Brad began talking to Darren. Rick stood at the back of the van. I saw him take something from his pocket and slide it into the van. Then his hand slipped back into his pocket. What had he done? He and Brad wished Darren luck and left.

As soon as their backs were turned, I looked into the van. Things looked OK. Nothing had been taken. I was puzzled. Near the door was the yellow pedal — the one Darren uses most. I picked it up. It was stiff.

The pedals have to move up and down
easily. I turned it over. It was full of putty.
The pedal would not work.

Right Brad, I thought. You asked for it.

"You want to come with us, Lisa?" Darren
asked.

"Try and stop me," I said. I jumped into the van. On the way, I scraped the putty out of the pedal. By the time we pulled up at the Town Hall it was working again.

Chapter Six

Turning the tables

At the Town Hall I helped the boys unload. All the other bands were doing the same. Backstage was a mess. There were cords and gear all over the place. Sophy and the Songbirds were there. They wore shiny blue dresses.

Brad and Rick came up. I could see their guitars near the wall. Brad's guitar was a big black one. There are screws on the end of a guitar. They keep the strings in tune. Brad and Rick began to talk to Sophy. Rick likes her. They were not looking at me.

I twisted all the screws on Brad's guitar. Now it was out of tune.

The Songbirds sang first. All the kids from school were at the back of the hall. They cheered and clapped. When their turn came, the Heartbeats played a new song that Darren had made up. It sounded great. Two other bands played. Then it was Brad's turn.

The prison-bar lights flashed on. Brad strode to the front of the stage. He began to play. But at the first note he nearly dropped his guitar. The music sounded awful! Brad did not know what was wrong. He took a step back.

There was a man in the front row with mohawk hair. "Don't rattle your chain! It's not feeding time yet!" he shouted.

"You shut up," Brad snapped back. He forgot about the microphone.

"Shut up! Shut up!" went all around the hall. People began to boo and whistle.

"You come and make me," yelled the mohawk.

Brad took a swing at him with the guitar. Rick ran to help. He tripped over the ball and chain and landed on top of the mohawk.

Now everyone was laughing. People stood on chairs to see. They began to chant, "Take them off! Take them off!" The whole hall joined in.

The Chain Gang was done for.

Sophy and the Songbirds won the Battle of the Bands. Darren did not mind. A man from a record company was in the hall. He asked Darren to make a record for his company. So Darren won, too, in a way.

And Brad? Well, he got what he deserved. Nothing.